AF413820

FROM REVERIE TO REQUIEM

SUBBAIAH NM

To kutti Subbu, here's to you.

Contents

Contents

Foreword – I

In *From Reverie To Requiem,* Subbaiah takes readers on a profound journey through the depths of thought and emotion. Though young in years, his voice carries the weight of old questions and new wonder, of dreams dreamt and griefs endured, of love blossoming and life lived. These are not just poems, but rather, are revelations- unfolding slowly, line by line, like a dusk sky deepening into stars.

Subbaiah's unique ability to weave intricate imagery with poignant emotion sets him apart as a poet of exceptional promise. Each verse is a testament to his deep connection with the world- its beauty, its challenges and the quiet moments of grace often overlooked.

There really is something very captivating in his ability to render both the whimsical and the wounded with equal care. His language does not strain for meaning- it arrives, quietly, like memory returning from a time long forgotten, imbuing within it the essence of human experiences and relationships in ways that feel both deeply personal and universally relatable.

Readers will notice that Subbaiah does not shy away from the darker corners of existence, but his poetry is never without hope, not the naive kind but earned— a beacon of resilience and faith in the face of adversity.

These poems remind us of the power of words to heal, inspire and transform— offering readers not merely verses to flip through, but a companion and guide through life's trials and tribulations. Afterall,

"*Why worry about dead yesterdays or unborn tomorrows when today is so beautiful, so sweet?*"

May this young poet continue to grow in his craft, scaling new heights while remaining true to his voice and vision. His work is a gift, and I am confident it will leave an indelible mark on all who read it.

God bless you, Subbaiah, let this be the first of many offerings!

Shobha Subbaiah Monnanda
Author, Poet, Historian
Kodag

Foreword – II

When I first met Subbaiah N.M., I did not merely meet a student of Law — I encountered a presence. A quiet resilience wrapped in humility, a fierce intellect softened by compassion, and above all, a spirit that had weathered life's fiercest tempests and emerged illumined.

As Director of the School of Law at CHRIST University, I have witnessed many bright minds walk through our corridors but rarely does one leave behind a trail that is incandescent, and indelible.

Subbaiah's poetry collection, *From Reverie To Requiem,* is not just a testament to artistic brilliance. It is an act of survival, a hymn of defiance, a meditation on light and loss, and ultimately, a profound celebration of life. Every verse in this volume pulses with a quiet urgency- a longing to make sense of suffering, and an unwavering gaze toward beauty, even in the bleakest of moments.

In the poem *"The Light of the ONE,"* Subbaiah dares to voice the kind of questions most would not even whisper- questions about divine light, faith and the fragility of our fates:

"Oh! can we depend on the HOLY ONE for their luminous light?

Or are our fates sealed shut away / like a plant from the morning light?"

There is no easy theology here, only a wrestling faith- one born not in sanctuaries but in hospital rooms, not in certainties but in the fragile hope of each dawn.

And yet, alongside this existential grappling, Subbaiah offers glimpses of wonder. *"Illuminate"* reads like a cosmic revelation:

"They saw the birth of love, the whispers of dreams, from silent tears to joyous gleams…"

A verse that seems to breathe with the rhythm of creation itself. The sheer scale of imagination — the marriage of the micro and the infinite, speaks to a poet whose soul has wandered among stars and scars alike.

And in *"The Wicked Weaver,"* the haunting lines—

"The weaver feasts on me, my very bone it breaks,/my flesh, it rends…"

—offer a brutal honesty about pain and mortality. Yet even in the shadow of Promethean suffering, Subbaiah's voice does not falter. It sings, cries, confronts and endures. It is a voice that refuses to yield— and in that refusal, it finds its own kind of redemption.

Beyond the pages of this book, Subbaiah continues to shine as a sharp Legal thinker and an empathetic classmate, whose insights into jurisprudence and justice reflect the same sensitivity and depth that run through his poems. His ability to straddle the rigour of Legal argument and the vulnerability of poetic expression is not just rare— it is extraordinary.

This collection, then, is more than a student's offering; it is a life lived in fierce awareness, a journey from reverie to requiem and back again. I believe readers will find themselves gently undone by its beauty, stirred by its courage and awakened by its truths.

It is with deep admiration and pride that I commend this book to you.

May its light reach you, as it has reached all of us who know the luminous being that is Subbaiah N.M.

Fr. Thomas T.V.
Director, School of Law
CHRIST (Deemed to be University), Bangalore

Author's Note

Ah. It's done. It's finally complete. I've published my first book and written my second one too! (Credit to my 10-year-old self for that one- it's coming someday.)

So… what now? Do I dive into the next one, or sit back, relax a while and just take my time? I guess I'll let you— my readers— decide that, based on how you feel about this book.

What is this about, you ask? Well… Poetry.

I've always thought that poetry exists for everyone. Somewhere, somehow, there's a kind of poem out there for every person. My goal was to write that kind of poetry- something that might resonate with anyone. So, in this book, you might find poems you love, some you skip, maybe even a few you abhor…and, who knows, one or two that might make you snore. You know what I'm saying?

I'm not writing to please— I'm writing to inspire. To show that you can build a legacy of your own.

Sounding a bit corny? Maybe. But hey— I was strictly instructed to include a "purpose" behind this book. And while I could come up with some big, lofty reason, the truth is, I just wanted to put something out into the world that I could call my own. A little selfish? Maybe. But I'm just a bit grandiose like that… ;)

This is a book for everyone. A story. A journey through how I've felt and thought over the years- about love, nature, spirituality, pain and more. You may relate. You may not. But after you've read this, I hope you'll feel what I've felt— at least once in your own life. So go on, start flipping through the pages.

And now, my acknowledgements.

Thank you, my *Karonas,* my ancestors, for the blessings showered on me.

Thank you, my wonderful parents for your love and support in getting this book out there. Especially my mother, for always pushing me forward despite my selective procrastination (Don't whack me, Ma. Thank you), and my father, for being my pillar of strength, through everything.

To my mentor, my grandmother, thank you for inspiring me to commit to this journey in the first place, and for being a forever sweetheart all these years.

To my Department Director at Law school, Fr. Thomas, thank you for being a constant source of encouragement and for supporting me so kindly. Many of these poems were written during my time here, and your quiet faith in me helped make them possible.

Huge thanks to my dear friends, Samrudh, Deon and Pranay, for patiently reading draft after draft, and providing valuable feedback, *even though I pestered you all endlessly.* To Johan and Uncle Dax, for your nudge in making me get this book out. To Jeremy, for always letting me borrow some of your creativity. Last but not the least, to Rohit, for generously giving me the title for one of my best poems (I hope there is no claim for copyright infringement now, ahem).

And thank you, dear Reader, for picking up this book and giving me the chance to take you through this journey.

So here it is. My heart, in poems.

15

Thank you for reading—and Cheerio!

Subbaiah Nuchimanyanda Muthanna
Poet
From Reverie To Requiem

Troop El Gato

Delicate whiskers that gently caress,

Soft paw prints, adored on a pretty dress,

Different coats, shades and sheen,

An assorted color palette,

Calico, tux, white, ginger...not green!

Nudges, nuzzles, pats and pleads,

No remorse for their mischievous deeds,

Being so cute, it fulfills their needs,

Clearly, they're the masters and we, their steed.

Of dramatic hissing and rhythmic purrs,

Of matted fluff, laden with burrs,

Of continuous baths, to keep sleek their fur,

Of little critters and creatures as predators,

They lure.

Aloof they play about, in sparkling sunshine,

Their pompous joy at the sight of their favourite hoo-man,

Kind and benign,

A glint in their eyes, as they quickly spy—

A darting fly, fluttering leaf,

Or *even* thread, string or twine.

They're creatures of mystery, shadows and the Night,

The mesmerizing feline gaze, amber eyes gleaming bright,

To compare their charm, their devilish charisma—

It'd be trite,

Best appreciate their elegance, being graceful as a sprite.

Curled up in corners, where sunlight streams,

Lost in their own world, the midst of their dreams,

To be this casual, it's as bold as it seems,

Their smiles, sly, with a Cheshire gleam.

The flick of a tail, a twitch of a nose,

Silent and stealthy, they strike successive blows,

Their targets are felled, with unnerving force,

Be it bugs, mice or a flock of doves.

From ancient Egypt to our homes of today,

Their regal presence has never gone away,

Worshipped as gods, to Bast we'd prayed,

A timeless affection, one that'd never sway.

They leap and they bound, with agility so rare,

Climbing high places, defying gravity, with style and flair,

Chasing their own shadows, playful without care,

Bounding through gardens in gusto—

They'd *even* fight a bear!

Their purrs are a symphony, a soothing hum,

A balm for the soul, like the subtle beat of a drum,

They curl up beside you, these balls of fur, soft as a plum,

A gentle reminder of their hypnosis however,

Your heart strings they'd surely strum.

With whiskers twitching, they sense all around,
Alert to the slightest, faintest sound,
Their world is a wonder, endlessly vast and round,
They stand at the top, kings proudly crowned.

From kittens to elders, their spirits remain,
Independent and curious, with a streak of the arcane,
In every pounce, power to slay their bane,
Possessing hearts of lions, their enemies' courage lay drained.

Their companionship is simple, no need to impress,
Just being with them, relieves of all of life's stress,
They bring us joy, in their subtle, sly way,
A reminder to cherish them, each and every day.

In our homes and hearts, they've carved their niche,
Not just as pets, but family, filling life's breach,
With their quirks and charms, they're here to stay,
A testament to love, in their own special way.

Their meows, their mews— tuned in lagato,
In their colonies, they've settled, as Troop El Gato!

Howdy Ho! A Gambit's Gone Awry

There once lived a man who lost all that he had,

The grimmest of days, in sobriety he lay clad,

How'd it happen? — it was all too quick,

He'd been robbed clean, by a smart ol' chick.

She'd swiftly swept him off his feet,

Taken all his booze, had him beat,

The man was left without a choice to make,

A victim of his own terrible mistake.

His story began as the clock struck six,

The boozer, filled with a varied mix,

Our protagonist, a man of a sullen soul,

Lingering about at this watering hole.

He'd seen her enter from across the bar,

Their eyes locked, as he'd looked from afar,

A gaze so condescending, it'd left him spurned,

To show face, he so eagerly yearned.

Stood on his chair, pointed at her he did,

"You're too prim, too proper, I challenge you to a bid!"

Only a wager he'd thought and he bet it all,

"A game of Cards! Accept, if you have the gall!"

Gladly she joined, a challenge was made,

"I am a master of my craft!" with pride he'd say.

But little did he know of her wily skill,

How she'd win by trickery, with her devious will.

He shuffled the cards, his hand so steady,

Thinking himself as being shrewd, so sure and ready,

But she played the game with such finesse and flair,

Her innocent smile had thrown him off—

He was in her snare.

However he tried, he couldn't believe,

The outlandish hands she'd won,

The deceitful webs she'd woven.

Each card laid down was a stroke of fate,

Sealing his doom, for it was far too late.

The woman, all the while, sat grinning,

For he hadn't seen how she'd been sinning,

Each hand she won, she took a prize,

Emptying his pockets, with her facetious lies.

But little did she know, the man had a plan,

He was not quite the charade he'd played—

Of being the simple man,

He'd let her win, played the fool,

To set up a trap, so vicious and cruel.

He had lured her close, with a wager so sweet,

A final hand, where the stakes would meet,

Everything he had, he laid out on the table,

A last chance to win, if she was able.

Her greed now blinding, she lost her steam,

Not knowing his loss was part of a grand scheme,

As she revealed her hand with a boastful cheer,

The man's eyes gleamed, for his victory was near.

He flipped his cards with a wicked ol' grin,

Revealing the ace that sealed his brilliant win,

The woman gasped, her face now pale, aghast,

Her reign of deceit had ended, at last.

Caught in her greed, she lost it all,

From riches to ruin, she'd made her fall,

And the man walked away, his head held high,

For he'd won by his wit, not by a lie.

So, here's a lesson for all who like to play,

Fortunes can change, in fascinating ways,

Never underestimate your opponent, your foe,

For you never know just how far they'll go.

In the end, it's the strategic and smart,

Who outwit the cheaters-at-heart,

A game well-played, a tale well-spun,

The trickster had been tricked—

Justice had won.

A Dear One's Perfume

With vibrant yet humble attire,

She stands with an arm outstretched,

Beckoning her children close,

And her grandchildren, closer.

Her sanguine presence,

Matched with the wafting scent

of her perfume,

Calming and washing off us,

Our worry and discontentment.

A blend as divine as this,

Would be impossible to find,

A comparison inexplicable,

No material object

could fulfill.

Adored for never shying away,

When it came to dispensing her love,

To her, it was all but exhausting,

Only naysayers would think otherwise.

Her scent, a tapestry of memories,

Interwoven with threads of time,

Each note— a whisper of past joys,

A reminder of her gentle nature,

Her adventurous prime.

In the warmth of her embrace,

We find solace, peace, space,

She provides a sanctuary from life's race,

Where all troubles cease to exist—

To set our footing,

Right in place.

Her delicate perfume lingers in the air,

It stands proof of her elegant flair,

Principled, wise, beyond compare,

Values that echo her loving soul,

A rarity, in this world,

A resource so scarce.

Through seasons and years gone by,

Her essence remains the same,

A constant under every sky,

Her presence—

A beacon with an eternal flame.

She carries stories within her scent,

Of laughter, tears, dreams—

A life lived with no relent,

One where love engulfs,

Encompasses you whole,

Flowing like a gentle stream.

In her presence, we find our home,

A place of warmth and light,

No matter where we roam,

Her love remains our guiding sight.

So, we gather near, and closer,

In the circle of her embrace,

grateful for every moment—

Each we hold dearer,

Bound, by her perfume,

Her virtue,

Her endless grace.

Canines in Cahoots

Bristling tufts of fur, playful gaits,

Paw prints on the sidewalk,

Fresh with paint,

Stock, breeds and colors,

From black to white,

Flashy in motion,

Golden, speckled,

Zooming without fright.

Whimpers and yearns, their royal pleads,

Their endless charm and their endless needs,

With wagging tails, their joy precedes,

They're not just pets, but our partners indeed.

Of barking out loud and silent growls,

Playful tussles and midnight howls,

Of muddy paws and flopping jowls—

Fetching sticks, chasing fowl.

Bounding through fields under the sunny sky,

Their joyous stomps as we pass by,

A glint in their eye, a spark so spry,

As they spot a squirrel, a cat, or a bird up high.

Our companions by day, our guardians by night,

Their protective stance, a fearless sight,

To describe their loyalty, all words fall slight,

Praise their bravery—

The canine moxie, shining bright!

Snuggling by us, their warmth abounds,

Lost in dreams of running rounds,

Their siestas, their rest— timeless,

Without bounds,

Their smiles so broad, it'd surely astound!

A wag of their tails, a droop to their ears,

Their presence felt close, they're always near,

Their hunts are swift, not a semblance of fear,

Be it ball or bone, no trophy is mere.

From ancient hunts to modern play,

Their spirit endures, come what may,

Partners in history, in every fray,

Their bond with us—

It shall never sway.

Running wild and amok, with energy so rare,

To dirty our mint furniture, they'd definitely dare,

Chasing their own tail without a care,

Through gardens and parks, they'd jump about,

Giving our poor hearts a good ol' scare.

Their barks are a chorus, a familiar sound,
A melody of joy, when we're around,
They snuggle close, their love is so profound,
A constant comfort,
In them, always found.

With keen senses, they stand their ground,
Alert to the slightest, softest sound,
Their world is us, just us, all around,
Their loyalty, unmatched—
Forever to stay strong.

With mischief and fun, their spirits glow,
Adventurous and playful, wherever they go,
In every bark, in every woof,
Their love they'd show,
With hearts of gold, their bravery,
They bestow.

Their companionship is so pure and true,
No need to impress, they love all of you,
They bring us joy, in ways so new,
A reminder, once more, to cherish them,
In everything we do.

In our homes and hearts, they've carved their place,

Again, not just as pets, but a loved one's place,

With their quirks and charm, they set the pace,

A tribute to love, we're the King to their Ace.

Naughty, sweet, caring, to boot,

In danger, in trouble, they stand astute,

Together they band— Canines in Cahoots,

A tie so strong,

Their love is absolute.

My Moonshine Succour

She basks in the lucent crescent glow,

Wrapped in a silhouette of serene delight,

Adorned in a silvery, lustrous sheen,

A dream that reality materialized,

Beneath the dark, obsidian night.

Her gown, a cascade of quiet space,

Each crease, a tale of timeless grace,

Her touch, a felt of tender care,

Each fold of her palm—
Soft as a butterfly's cocoon,
More magical, than a runic lair.

Her presence is a symphony unsung,
Of calm, of warmth, of moonlight spun,
Unsullied she is, a profound hymn,
Of beauty, pure and sublime within.

Her cheeks blush, red as a dusky flame,
Her eyes, deep as twilight's tender wane,
At her sight, no mortal remains sane,
She is my moonshine succour—
Reliever of my pain.

Her lips, like velvet, a soft embrace,
But sweet as poppies, bestowing Heavenly grace,
Her skin, a treasure a craftsman would seek,
The ultimate dream toward achieving his peak.

She is the union of the earth and the eventide,
A shining diamond, forever by my side,
Fleeting she lies, like a bloom of rose and peach,
Whispering secrets that lie just out of reach.

Her voice possesses a cadence as light as air,

Her each word uttered, equal to a divine prayer,

And with her each phrase spoken,

I've fallen into an enchanting snare—

A melody that would soothe the frayed,

Make even a hardened heart begin to care.

She speaks, and all the world stands still,

Beguiled, surrendering to her grit and will,

Her smile, a beacon in the pitch-dark,

A flint that lights a dazzling spark,

It speaks of her kindness stark,

My heart does long for her—

Singing as does a euphonic lark.

She crafts a haven with her shimmering glow,

Where only love and trust are said to grow,

A moonshine that dances brilliantly,

Like a phoenix flame,

Drawing you close, binding your soul—

Where no heart is left untouched,

Where no life stays the same.

For *even* Venus pales in compare,

Her heart laden with rue,

Her moonlit charm eclipses all,

Except the worthy few,

My heart, it falters for her—

An arrhythmic beat,

As her essence envelops me,

I wish it would all repeat.

A brazen tempest churns within my chest,

Even still, she soothes my heart to rest,

Her being, it's a paradox whole and complete,

Both a chaos wild and a calm retreat.

For in her lunar wake the world feels new,

Like a canvas fresh, with vibrant hues,

The tides now churn, as my love does pine,

Where no myth shall speak, no verses define,

The spellbound glow she emanates—

Her seraphic moonshine.

To chase her is to lose the day,

Finding her is to fade away,

Yet I walk, though I am led astray,

A willing pawn in her astral ballet.

And so, beneath her silver reign,

I yield my heart, my soul, my name,

All to the queen of the endless night,

The crescent reprieve to my fated plight—

My moonshine succour, my marble dame,

The bearer of my signet, holder of my name.

My Love, My Light, My Luminary

Amidst any and all turmoil,

She stands unfettered, beyond the need to toil,

A figure of strength, with great power,

At whose conviction, *even* the brave would cower.

She walks with elegance, an effortless stride,

A calm demeanor, immense pride by her side,

Her charisma and aura- boundless, grand,

With intelligence so sharp, only a few can withstand.

Her teachings and lessons, writings so fine,

Embedded in history, like rich, aged, delicious wine,

Every word she speaks, a treasure, a gem,

As invaluable as her signature and her emblem.

Her stories, a trove where wisdom does glow,

Equal to the love she does constantly show,

With fervor and might, she urges me to see,

Never to bow to anyone or anything,

To enjoy life to its fullest, to the T.

Against swift Fjords, gigantic Alps and the vast Seas,

Her strength inspires, urging me to be free,

To face the world with courage untold,

With her loving embrace, forever to hold.

For her, I'd strive to be more than just better,

Her every hug and every kiss,

So soothing, leaving my heart aflutter,

I love you so much more than what mere words can tell,

My love for you, so endless, in abundance,

Equalling a force that not *even* the Heavens can quell.

So, here's to you, my dearest Grandmother,

For shaping me up, making me exactly as I must be,

I'll continue to hold on to you—

My pillar of strength, the source of my glee.

Within the depths of my heart and soul,

Your essence as my dear one's perfume,

It's fulfilled its set-out goal

To fill me with joy and happiness so profound,

That my smile shines brighter,

Brighter than the North Star all year round!

My love, my light, my luminary,

I wish you joy and elation,

Sweeter than the sweetest cherry.

A Splash of Emerald & Green

The Earth, a sprawling kingdom, vast and wise,

Embraces forest princesses that reach for the skies,

Emerald gowns of leaves in dappled light, they wear,

Crowns of jewels that dance under the sunbeams' care.

Whispering pines, stoic oaks, with roots deep and strong,

Guardians of secrets where ferns and moss belong,

A hidden brook flows, identical to a silverworm that softly
crawls,

Through shadowy bristling groves, where sunlight
gently falls.

Here, humans seek solace under leafy shades wide,
Finding strength in weathered stone, a seasoned sculptor's pride,
Poets listen to the forest's song, their hearts synced in rhyme,
Hunters frolic about in nature's dance, losing track
of their time.

Life and death lay entwined, in nature's sacred trance,
A cycle of rebirth, of renewal, where all find their chance,
The forest freely gives, no wish is left denied,
Wood for shelter, warmth from fire, life's spirit—
Amplified.

Fruits and herbs, a bounty from the skies' sweet embrace,
A sanctuary for souls seeking shelter, within this beautiful place,
A silent pact made, a bond of respect deeply sown,
In the heart of every visitor—
A witness to dear nature's reverence grown.

We tread with care upon this hallowed ground,
Where emerald guardians stay abound,
With whispers of old times, the quiet wisdom does show,
These Forest princesses- Earth's guardians,
Adorned in nature's grace, our patronage in tow.

Beneath the canopies lie tales of creatures small and great—

From nimble squirrels to majestic bears,
destined to share an emerald fate,

Echoes of hoofbeats and birdsong's sweet refrain,

Each, a part of the symphony—
The forest's endless, melodic chain.

In every rustle of leaves and every gust of breeze,

A story unfolds, more ancient, abstruse, than the very trees,

Roots intertwined, reaching deep into the earth,

An unseen network, evidence to nature's worth.

With every step we take, a footprint left behind,

In the soft earth, observed, a quaint reminder of humankind,

May our presence here be gentle, like a waning tide's crest,

To care for the emerald canvas, the memories, we have made best.

For the forest lives on, in whispers soft and clear,

Guiding us, reminding us, why we hold it so dear,

In its emerald embrace, we find our sacred space,

Amongst the forest princesses, our kindred—
Nature's timeless grace.

The Light of the One

The wind blows rough,

The sails, flying—

Moving side to side

on the verge of tearing away.

Regrettably as if,

The Northern Wind,

was steering our ship

to the storm's wake.

Mayday! Mayday!

Is there a chance today

for us all to remain?

The wind blows longer still

and the ship's flooding persists.

Oh!

Can we depend on the Holy One,

for their lustrous light?

Or are our fates sealed,

Shut away like a plant

from the morning light?

Seemingly,

out of nowhere,

brightly shone a light,

But alas—

Not from the Heavens.

Grim, we thought,

as were our chances,

and eerily,

as how the light seemed.

It was not the Holy One's,

But rather, an unknown figure's,

Yet we,

still continued our prayers,

and did so, to be safe.

But this light was The One,

The One, that saved us,

guided us,

from the storm's wake.

How thankful were we,

for our ship's and our sakes,

Smitten were we,

by this faux

of Heavenly Grace.

However, the light still unknown,

is one we pray to,

as well as,

Fear every day.

As mysterious as it was,

It still was The One,

that steered us clear,

from the storm's wake.

Eventually, we were,

shielded and sheltered—

free from despair.

Waiting for

the winds to mellow,

To be—

Safe to sail again.

Serenity's Embrace

In the depths of a restless soul,

Where tumultuous waves once crashed,

There now reigns a tranquil calm,

A stillness that forever lasts.

Like a gentle stream's soft murmur,

Or a breeze that whispers through the trees,

Peace has found its dwelling place,

In the heart that now feels at ease.

No longer does the mind wander,

In search of answers yet untold,

For in the quietude of this moment,

All mysteries gently unfold.

The chaos of the world outside,

Fades to a distant, muted sound,

As the inner self finds solace,

In the peace that it has found.

Simply said, this inner peace,

Tugs the strings of your soul,

Like the ebbing warmth of a newborn hearth,

With red, golden, glistening coals.

No storm can shake this inner peace,

No darkness dims its radiant light,

Akin to a beacon in the night,

A guiding star, it shines, forever bright.

So let this peace be your companion,

Through all the trials and the strife,

And you shall find, within yourself,

The true meaning of life.

Let serenity be your guide,

In the journey that lies ahead,

And you shall find, in its embrace,

The calmness of a soul, well-fed.

Illuminate

It'd all started simply with a Bang,

One so mighty, so powerful,

The darkness'd shied away,

T'was but the Supreme One's,

own hand,

That created the skies,

and the lands.

It filled the vessel of the cosmos,

With a blazing sight—

One so ancient,

Mere mortals could not handle,

One so extreme,

Almost mistaken,

as being celestial vandals.

On such a vast canvas, their Odyssey began,

To rid all of Creation, of its every blight,

Birthed to fit such design, were indeed the Stars,

The Supreme One's very own,

Perfect shining knights.

The Stars continued with their roles,

To fill fragments with parts of their lustrous souls,

To grant them their wishes of peace, serenity—

Fill them with satisfaction, pure serendipity.

Left to Illuminate for eternity and longer,

The Stars, looking after their creations,

Quietly pondered,

They questioned their purpose, their celestial right,

Seeking knowledge, what lay yonder,

Beyond the Supreme One's cosmic might.

As ages passed and Time'd unfold,

The Stars watched over it all,

Even the stories untold—

Witnessing worlds in their celestial dance,

From the rise of empires to the fall of chance.

They saw the birth of love, the whispers of dreams,

From silent tears to joyous gleams,

From cosmic dust to sentient life,

All seen under the Stars' watchful light.

The Stars' glow brings the shadows of Night,

Darkness' existence, it came from the light,

Like Yin and Yang, the two are intertwined,

Embrace both, as Van Gogh opined,

In his masterpiece, The Starry Night.

The Stars embraced both joy and sorrow,

Guiding all to every new tomorrow,

In their brilliance, kind wisdom was found,

In their shimmering constellations, truths are unbound.

The Stars remained a timeless guide,

In the boundless universal expanse,

The eternal tide.

So, they shine, forever bright,

Guardians of the day, keepers of the night,

Ever grateful to the Supreme One,

For the gift to sparkle, dream, illuminate—

A truly divine sight.

Illuminate, they did and still do,

Casting hope with every hue,

A reminder in the endless cosmic sea,

Of the immense power of divinity.

A Mother's Boon, A Mother's Bane

In the fields of green, where flowers dance,

The Mother's Boon lies, in a gentle trance,

Her nurturing touch, a soothing balm,

In her embrace, all'd find peace and calm.

Yet in her depths, lies a hidden strain,

The Mother's Bane, her whispered pain,

Her rivers lay choked, her forests solemnly weep,

In her sorrow, her secrets, she must tightly keep.

The duality of her gentle grace,

The burden she heavily bears, there is but a trace,

We tread upon her with our careless feet,

Unaware, the balance lies constrained—

So utterly delicate, so utterly fleet.

Cherish her gifts, we must,

With reverence, credulous and deep,

Heal her wounds, we must, before we sleep,

For in her love, and in all her strife,

Lies the supreme essence, to all of life.

With every waking dawn, a new chance given,

To mend ties, so harshly riven,

To plant the seeds of hope and care,

In fields, in plains, in forests—

Everywhere.

Her mountains stand forlorn, a silent plea,

Honor her! Lest her wrath compels you to flee!

Her oceans vast, with secrets so old,

Stories of life, in wait, yet to be told.

From the tiniest sprout to the most towering tree,

Each part of her sings in euphonic harmony,

But when we forget, when we neglect,

Her cries of anguish, we must expect.

For every plastic shard, each poisoned stream,

Mars her beauty, her chances of achieving her dream,

Yet hope remains, if we unite,

To restore her glory, to make all things right.

With every hand that lifts to sow,

A future very bright, begins to grow,

Let kindness lead, let wisdom guide,

In every beating heart, let lush love reside.

In honoring her, we honor ourselves,

For her health reflects our very cells,

The Mother's Boon, the Mother's Bane—

Two sides of a coin, both joy and pain.

So let us vow, with hearts held sincere,

To protect the Earth that we hold so dear,

For in her balance and in her grace,

Lies the future of our human race.

Empty it Was, Empty it Shan't Be

I feel a space within my heart,

One that has not been filled—

A void awaiting,

A name, a possession, a feeling,

To envelop,

With tender emotion and warm embrace.

This space, it follows me,

For I have wandered far too long,

Leaving it barren, plain,

Like a nightingale, stripped of song.

It pulls me to act,

Yet I lack the will, the courage,

To fulfill its deep desires,

To satisfy it, for eternity.

When will I learn?

When will I believe?

When will I understand—

That this is how I must proceed?

I realise now this space exists,

Because of me—

Alas, I must change my ways,

Honor it as it truly desires,

And as it truly needs.

I feel the weight of its silent plea,

Echoing through my veins—

A reminder of what could be,

If only I would change.

I yearn to fill this space,

To grant it peace, rest,

To nurture it with care, with love,

To give it my very best.

But fear holds me back,

A shadow over my intent,

Preventing me from moving forward,

From being truly content.

I must face this fear,

Embrace the unknown path,

For only then will I find solace,

And fill this waiting space.

With every step, I'll learn to trust,

To release my forlorn past,

To open up my weary heart,

Cleanse my grieved soul—

Find love that truly,

Lasts.

So I will change my ways,

Act on pure intent, desire,

To envelop this space with all I am,

To light it with my brilliant fire.

In this journey I'll find resolve,

To be free,

The strength to live a life,

Full and bright—

To be the best of me.

I will leave no stone left unturned,

No path untaken,

No wrong left uncorrected,

No doubt left without clarity.

For in embracing this journey,

I will find peace and tranquility,

Whole, unbroken—

A life without regrets,

With every space left empty.

Not as a void, or unfathomable gorge,

But a canvas,

Waiting to be filled,

With what must be.

Trophy of Horrors

Escaped from ignorance and into our Grace,
You, who we are glad to humbly embrace,
Staving off the evil and horrors from yourself,
Have you decided yet to join our forbidden faith?

Do you intend to attend our episode,
Our proceedings of utmost belief,
An impression we are required to make,
As you continue to lie in our wake?

This path, chosen, have you yet?

Do you choose to stay by us or,

To run away from your fate?

Petrified, are you, to deal,

With the demons themselves?

Do you, with certainty, dare challenge us?

With enough gut,

To prove that you will make the cut—

Being the one to lift the accolade!

Enter our realm, where shadows dwell,

Where secrets whisper and darkness swells,

Do you fear the trials that lie ahead?

Or will you conquer your very dread?

With courage, step into our world,

Where nightmares are unfurled,

Face the horrors, face the fright,

Prove your mettle in the night.

The echoes of torment, the cries of despair,

Will you withstand, will you dare?

To claim the trophy, to rise above,

To embrace the darkness,

To conquer with love.

This journey demands your soul's fire,

A heart unyielding, a fierce desire,

To confront the terrors, to face the night,

To emerge victorious, with newfound might.

For only those who brave the abyss,

Who confronts their fears, do not miss,

Will earn the honor, the ultimate prize,

The trophy of horrors, in dark disguise.

So, decide now, your fate is near,

Will you stand strong, will you persevere?

Or turn away and flee in fright,

From the challenge that lies in this twilight.

Embrace our faith, join our creed,

Prove your worth, fulfill our need,

To rise above, to claim your place,

In the hall of champions, in our sacred space.

Of Lethargy, Of Sloth, Of Fatigue

Despite passions blazing,

My dreams unfolding,

I can't help but notice,

The subtlety of my subconscious,

in preparing Me.

A whisper of sorts, almost untold,

So withdrawn, yet,

So expressive—

"Time will not wait, for long,

Beware your nature, of whiling"
Must I obey my unconscious?
Its warning, of my potential, waning,
My capability, failing,
My energy despairing?

The soulless chattering that persists,
What I once believed to be my thoughts,
Now but desist,
Any form of intelligible distinction,
And rather,
Perpetuate delusion and insanity,
That which I cannot resist.

A mellow pace of the senses,
The mental and physical,
Coalesced—
To be symbolic unity,
But bereft,
Of any principal,
Of any significance.

Alas,

Why must the will,

Of sloth,

Of lethargy,

Of fatigue,

Veil over my erudite canvas,

As I slip into this quandary,

Of immoral choices,

Unable to hold my stead,

Unable to stop, myself.

A mire of foggy thoughts remained,

They swamp my eccentric ego,

What earlier stood engulfed,

In fiery pride,

Now was but cindered—

The wafting charred scent,

Of my remnant pieces,

From the pyre I'd lit of my esteem—

A posthumous but brilliant blaze.

Escape this prison,

With haste I must,

Rise, as a phoenix does,

Enchant myself,

To change my very fate,

A Revenant, I must stand,

Lest the lethargy,

The sloth,

The fatigue,

Take my place.

A Pyrrhic Triumph

With the warm setting sun,

Came a simmered breeze,

By the sinking sands of the dune,

Where lay a sight at which,

Even shadows'd freeze.

There, by the arid field They stood,

Quiet, trembling, at their knees,

Languid, like decaying wood,

Their brows inadvertently creased,

Sweat dripping, their figures unkempt,

At a sight they'd never envisioned, or dreamt,

Bearing solemn guilt,

For the defeated, the vanquished and the deceased.

Many a rotting corpse, a stench of the End,

Many burnt bridges, never to mend,

Endless signs of the eerie,

At mercy to a phantom's pick,

Subject to visions so frightening,

Even the Brave'd bend,

Keeled over, to their stomachs—

Sullied, slovenly and sick.

A crimson hue emanating from the Victors,

The embodiment of their scorn,

A cruel, cold charade, chilling to the bone,

An ambience of pain all round,

The seeds of terror have been sown,

No stone left unturned—

For such loss,

They truly cannot atone.

Their brilliant intent, the design of their feats,

Now all but reduced,

To scattered flies,

Bawling eyes,

Bleak skies—

An epic so poignant,

The pen'd tremble to fill the sheets.

What purpose lay fulfilled?

What prophecy needed such blood spilled?

What conviction did They need,

To have their people meet their end,

Be killed?

There lies no solace, for they who are bested,

But neither does it lie, for the Victors,

And this battle that they've contested,

An insignificance for life,

Truly a force to be reckoned,

With their crude beliefs, it was inevitable—

Their demise, they'd clearly beckoned.

Alas, history has, but by the Victors, been made,

These tales of loss are merely empiric,

The conquered are left lost, vulnerable, afraid,

Bested of their tune, tone and lyric,

Devastation, havoc, ruin and degrade—

To the victors too, this triumph has stood,

As Pyrrhic.

A Haunted Summer

Surely there exists no dearth,

To this monochromatic overtone,

As lies a sight so eerie to take glimpse of,

Accompanied by the whispers of that,

Which once had flown.

The blistering heat, renowned far and wide,

As a sign of gaiety and the casual,

Now but a transfiguration of fear,

A fear of all but the factual.

The hours of Day now extended,

Giving the creature purpose, as it held back,

In wait.

The tranquility of light overshadowed,

By the shrieks of this sinister belligerent.

With every trickling drop of sweat,

Comes about a feeling of dread.

For thundering was the chimaera's call,

My body, red and disheveled, it lay,

As slowly but surely, I bled red.

And so, the story goes—

In the stillness of the summer night,

Echoes a primordial's tale,

Of terror, of hidden fright,

Where shadows dance with eerie grace,

Where whispers carry through empty space,

At a pace so profound, to leave any and all,

Fearful, and pale.

The once-familiar landscape has transformed,

Into a realm of nightmares, unadorned,

As the sunlit moon casts a ghastly glow,

On primal horrors that slyly lurk and grow.

A chill in the air, not from summer's breeze,

But from the presence that seeks to seize,

Every quivering, shaky breath taken,

Every twitch in the body, panic-stricken.

Where a fluttered beat of the heart,

Is one's sign to depart,

From summer's nocturnal balm,

Where malevolent darkness imparts.

The rustle of leaves, a sinister song,

The creak of branches, where shadows throng,

A symphony of fear, played during the brief night,

In this haunted season, basked in light.

And as the night wears in, on its cloak,

The unknown terrors, from their slumber, awoke,

The veil between the worlds grows thin,

Enter a gateway to this dreary realm,

Where roses bloom, curling black and grim.

Fear the summer stillness, its quietude,

For in its midst, lurks something crude,

A symbol of malice, a wicked dream,

A presence, ancient, a force unseen.

Within this sultry domain,

Nothing is as it'd seem,

So, beware of this demonic season,

Where even in the brightest light,

Only fear reigns supreme.

The Pain of Emotion

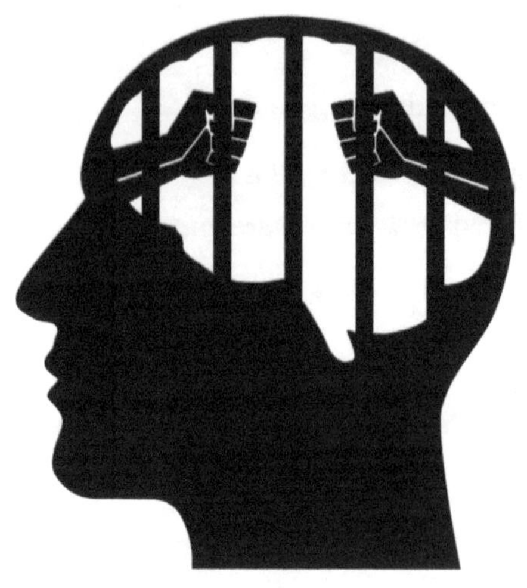

It has broken my heart,

Torn my mind apart,

Shaken me to my core,

And has me banging vigorously,

On the door.

I've cried too much,

I say, enough!

At my own behest,

I can do so no more.

All tears of mine have fallen,

Like incessant rain.

This madness of mine,

I bear witness to,

Delivering me untimely suffering,

And pain.

I'm stumbling, tripping,

And slowly falling,

Falling into a void,

Of no emotion.

All this noise, all this commotion,

What once there was,

Has now been replaced,

With emotion, silent and bare,

So empty,

Without conception.

My heart throbs,

My body quivers,

A feeling so despicable,

It's making me shiver.

I'm going cold,

And there's no way out,

The tears envelop me,

Dripping, like a spout.

The agony is subsiding,

It's time to regret,

Endure I must, for long,

So, it's better if I not fret,

Remembering the pain once more,

It's best that I forget.

Am I already out of time?

For I am losing all my breath,

With every sigh,

my spirit strains,

Tightly bound,

by invisible chains.

A spoken desire,

"Please, allay my fears!"

But, in vain,

My straits, much too dire—

The echoes of despair,

They persist!

Even the whispers numb,

Piercing like a wintry mist.

The world all over,

Moves so fast,

Yet here I stand,

Stuck in the desolate past—

The faces blur,

The voices blend,

A ceaseless cycle,

Without end.

But in this endless swathe of black,

This constant, dark rift,

I long deeply,

I long wholly,

For just a moment's bliss.

Where Are We Headed?

Of scorched earth and fiery auburn skies,

The masses still slumber, buried in devious lies,

Echoes of terror and carnage, carved into the land,

History remembers all—

Blood stains still etched in the sand,

Lands are being ravaged, wars still fought,

To bring an end to it all, must another angel's sacrifice,

At the stake, be sought?

Where are we headed?

Premonitions of decay and destruction are galore,

Hear Nature's cries, she can't take it anymore,

We've silenced her, poisoned her and hollowed out her core,
Stripped her of everything,

Leaving only the resentment she's stored,

The tides have risen, the winds have turned cold,

Yet, filled with hubris are we—

Unrelenting, arrogant, standing bold.

Where are we headed?

Propaganda stains the air we breathe,

People's voices- smothered by lullabies sung to deceive,

These savages still viciously thirst and crave—

For blood, battles and pillaging of *even* the graves,

Pursuing the ghastly intentions they'd adopted,

To turn a blind eye to the consequences, they've opted.

Where are we headed?

The chauvinists stand ruthless, with aggression they roar,

Bigotry festers in the silence— ignorance takes the floor,

As fragile egos are shattered, conflicts arise at
the slightest stir,

Societies acting as rabid as a mangy cur,

Disheveled, squalid, with flea-borne fur,

Truth, it's been left gutted, twisted, torn—

We must seek mercy, to be saved,

Lest we too like Truth, be mourned.

Where are we headed?

The machines built to lighten our grief, lessen our despair,

Now abet our complacency- we are addicted,

To comfort, to pleasure, to vice without care,

Progress has stagnated—our decay is imminent— beware!

There are no second chances, no Elysium to share.

Where are we headed?

We're trapped aboard a burning, sinking ship,

Curse the culprits- us- for striking the matches' tip,

It's a flame that we fed— let grow, let arc,

Doused in gasoline of a hatred we've been fed stark,

A likeness to Casabianca, we're stubborn to break free,

The cycle thus continues, an Armageddon it shall be.

Where are we headed?

There is no Father, saviour, nor savant, to safely guide,

Ready the funeral pyre, to our demise, we'll march and stride,

Only self-loathing shall linger over us, thick as stone,

Lest we bury our hatchets, hold a requiem to atone—

We're beyond the point where we can turn back,

Blame ourselves, we must, for the backbone we lack.

Where are we headed?

The flickering stars sear brilliantly,

As they pierce through the heavenly membrane,

The indication of havoc and calamity,

We bide our time to enter the sacred plane—

To make one last wish, one final plea,

To be saved from this self-inflicted pain,

Prevent an untimely demise that'd be much to our disdain.

Where are we headed?

Regret ricochets off the cocoon of comfort,

That we've veiled ourselves with,

Humanity is fated to be left in the dust—

Nothing, but a myth.

Where are we headed?

For You

For endless weary nights, awake I'd lay,

With thoughts bellowing, through and through,

My mind began to resent itself,

Unable to grasp,

How naive I'd stay, still hoping for something,

Despite how far apart we grew.

Neither the pitter-patter of the rain,

Nor the pelting scales of the storm outside,

The sweltering heat of the punishing sun, or,

The dusty breeze with its dampness now dried,

Could convince me that I'd follied,

That I'd left my sanity behind,

That I'd decided to pay the heavy price,

Of pain, of anguish, of chides.

I could not, nay, I would not ever believe,

How easily you lied,

How much you had to hide,

How flawed it seemed to be,

That even when you hurt me so deeply,

I sat down to listen, while to your heart's content,

You cried.

But my mind does not control me,

I stay true to my beating heart's score,

To me, you are still so beautiful, so pure, so green,

Somebody I so vehemently adore—

So much, that I'd still hold true,

All our experiences together,

In the little shelf I call my *Core*.

For you, I'd forget my mind,

For you, I'd leave everything behind,

For you, there are no loose-ends I wouldn't bind,

For you, there's no limit to being kind,

And for you, anything I'd jump right into—

Completely blind.

Not even the wear and tear of Eternity,

Shall lay stain on the memory,

That I've built of you, for you, to you—

For even if I ultimately cease to be,

I shall still hold true your bearing,

By way of an endless tryst,

With Time, with the Empty and,

With the Heavens themselves—

My love for you will persist.

There's no end to how much I accept you,

No end to how much I respect you,

How far I'd go,

How quick I'd run,

To you,

For you.

The Wicked Weaver

I see the shadowy silhouette of my fate,

As it rears its menacing, ugly head,

Its presence is thick—

A choking weight,

Like an evil spectre,

Waiting for its prey to find its bait.

The Weaver, it lies,

Jittery, impatient, in wait—

It waits where its shadow swallows all light,

Where whispers rot and dreams take flight,

Not of man, nor beast, with hunger it springs,

From voids unknown, with creeping, dark wings.

I see it calling out to me,

Its tone, of a wretched apathy,

A melody of doom, a mournful dirge,

It tries pulling me, deeper and deeper,

Into its dreadful purge.

To stake staunch claim to my being,

It threads the seams where hope still lay, freeing,

Forbidding me any joy, any empathy,

It leaves me stark and barren,

Stripped of any and all feeling.

I see it holding a clear crystal lens,

To judge me harsh, for many a deviant sin,

The Weaver, it peers at me with eyes of tar, tense,

Its web of ruin spun near and far—

Terribly dense.

It leaves no room for hope or prayer,

Only strands of despair, hanging in the air,

For I am, but to trudge along, to silently march,

To its wicked rhythm—

A harrowing song.

I, bereft of life's magic, am left trembling,

My soul stands paralyzed,

Its threads tightening, unrelenting,

Clutching, my body,

Clutching, my skin,

I let out a silent whisper of gratitude,

For my life as it once had been.

My thoughts, in consequence, are running amok,

It is a chaos I can barely contain—

I'm slowly going into shock,

Each step forward, my lips slip a cursed refrain,

Each breath taken, I remember,

A debt to repay,

Trust to regain.

The Weaver grins, its maw wide, agape,

Its promise is made clear- there is no escape,

My sins, my lies, are but within its loom,

It has woven my doom and is guiding me,

To my eternal tomb.

In its lair of marrow, rot and bone,

There is no generous mercy, no respite that is shown,

The crystal lens had revealed my flaws,

With my every secret exposed,
there is no escaping its jaws.

As my whimper rises, the Weaver lets it fall,

My whispers are in vain—

Pleas for mercy, met with its gall,

With guttural dismay, I shriek while I lay, small,

The Weaver watches, cold, indifferent, serene,

As its web gleams slick, with a malice keen.

And when the final thread is taut,

When every lie- forgot,

The Weaver descends with shrieking glee,

To feast upon me and my despair,

As I succumb to my misery.

I'd run if I could, but it knows my name,

My every move, my every shame,

Humming in wistful lament—

It knows I cannot fight,

Its shadow looms across, devouring all light,

My preservation is now a fallacy,

Lying just out of sight.

And as it drags me into its maw,

I gasp for air, to have one last breath to draw,

"Let me go, let me breathe, let me repent!"

But to my horror, the Weaver gleefully grins—

For its prey, ensnared, never wins.

Alas, no heroes have come, no songs have been sung,

My very shadow grips me, by my sins I am hung,

The Weaver feasts on me—

My every bone, it breaks, my flesh, it rends,

No matter my wishes nor my effort,

Like Prometheus, the pain just never ends.

The Silent Phone

The silent phone beckons one, beckons all,

You hear it ring- you pick it up, you speak,

But on the other end,

You wait and wait, and wait to hear—

No one. Nada. Nothing at all.

The silent phone, it listens to all:

Wishes, prayers, arguments—

Every kind of drivel,

Where does it go?

Who listens on the other end?

Questions that needn't be answered,

Answers that needn't be asked.

The silent phone, it keeps in touch,

Not by ringer, not by tune,

But by the wavelength it shares with you,

Your very own hum, you are its muse,

A spiritual beacon for it to peruse,

It listens to none else—

Only you.

And so, the silent phone remains,

A hollow mirror of our calls—

Transparent, for it has naught to share,

With you, with me, with anyone at all,

It reflects all that is spoken to it,

Yet, answers none.

Our whispers, held within its keep,

Our secrets, knotted quiet and deep,

No cracks to let the anguish seep—

It is an instrument, an echo chamber,

Nameless, claimless,

Yet remains wholly alive,

Even as we sleep.

And when at last we lay it down,

Its silence hums within our minds—

A gentle pulse, arrhythmic in its beat,

Or a deafening weight so great,

We can no longer bear it.

The silent phone, abstract as it seems,

Becomes the void, the space—

The place we seek to find ourselves,

Or one in which we are forever trapped,

Like a black abyss,

Vastly encompassing,

Without origin, without escape.

Cancer by Christmas

Beneath the frost of December's breath,

Lay great odds of a dance with death,

A race against time, many words left unsaid,

The frigid remains my only solace,

Against this terrible beast within me,

Blistering, bruising, burning my body red.

From joyful carols and twinkling lights,

Of living this season of love, pure and bright,

To now, a room gleamed in sterile, lifeless white,

Trapped, my spirit lies utterly crushed and in spite,

Reduced to a withered, ashen husk—

The malevolent handiwork of this wretched blight.

My weary soul beckoned the familial hearth,

Seeking consolation, I lay lamenting my birth,

Family, friends, white-coat strangers alike,

Filling the room with their chatter and chirp,

Their company, a placebo for my happiness,

For over narcotics, this I'd prefer—

This, I wouldn't shirk.

But tight-lipped, they were, about my fate,

Shrouded in the guilt of ignorance, of my pain,

Was it my body, that was my very foe?

Whatever it was, I was not allowed to know—

They didn't want to cause me more worry, nor woe,

Unaware that I was already marked,

By Death and it's scarlet glow.

In place of embellishing the Christmas tree,

Stringing together baubles, angels, lights,

In every shape, and in every form,

I bemoan as crooked fate has me bed-ridden,

Strung up to tubes and serrated contraptions—
A sorrowful scene, more so for the healthy,
Who are helpless to my suffering,
Who fail to grasp how the broken,
Are bound by their frailty.

A symphony of sickness emerged,
As the sounds began to crescendo—
Crying children,
Coughing elderly,
The flickering of dull lights,
The droning of machines,
The only remnants of the cold, dark nights—
Hellish episodes, for even the accustomed unwell.

Where the tinsel and decked halls glittered,
My poisoned blood clotted dark and thick,
Where joy bloomed in crimson ribbons,
Syringes like little harpoons pierced my skin,
Where gospels were sung in the Lord's faith,
I lay clasped within the anesthetic's cold embrace,
And where I quietly wished it'd all go away,
With reticence, an answer they'd say.

My vitals are vacillating, my pulse dropping,

I am stuck amidst a wavering sense,

Of serenity and ghastly unease,

Like Schrodinger's cat, living life in limbo,

My life slipping through my fingers,

Like thin, fragile strands of gossamer,

Leaving only my body's throes to be heard—

Fated to be carrion, fit to be scavenged.

Bruises of iridescent shades span my body,

My being, a guinea pig of procedures avant-garde,

With each passing cycle of chemo, I resign myself—

To the sheer pestilence,

To the pogrom of my cells from the inside out,

To the sedatives, for the chronic pain,

That I feebly tried to withstand,

Euthanasia would be an excellent gift,

But life is, alas, not that giving.

What I would give, to have the choice, the privilege,

Of wiping the tears streaming, dripping,

Down the creases of my face,

Over wiping blotches of my blood wedded,

To the hospital bed- dry, sticking,

Even the blots on my skin I'd tried to erase,

By swallowing peculiar pills, drinking sour syrups,

All the while, just watching, the struggle of tiny threads,

Holding together worn-out flesh—

My very own.

Wake up and smell the roses they said,

But why are the roses beside me,

Dried, shriveled, perishing,

Much like this body I once was pleased to call my own,

For left are tattered remains,

Of a normalcy I once cherished,

The life I'd dreamt of living for as long as alive I'd be,

Nothing but an empty wish,

Almost as facetious as a lunatic's fantasies.

But as the bleak days bled into dreary nights,

As hums replaced the holy midnight bells,

Somewhere in the hollow of my chest,

Amidst the congealed blood and the sedative haze,

A cindered flicker, a stubborn ember,

Buried deep beneath my ruined self,

Absolutely refused to die.

Not a roar, not a prayer, not a sermon of hope,

But the fragile breath of a soul that lay unsnuffed—

Mine

And *even* though my limbs hung about,

Like obelisks of sorrow, despair and,

Even though the mirror showed a specter, pale and scrawny,

A whisper rose to my lips where screams had ceased—

Live on, even if it is defiance, even if it is grief.

I began to count slowly,

Not the days left, but the days I'd endured,

Not the health that'd been siphoned away, that I'd lost,

But the pain that I'd weathered—

The pills had begun to taste bitter,

An aftertaste of rotten contempt,

My emotions, a ticking time-bomb,

Reluctant toward what lay before me, a dichotomy—

Do I find meaning in the nurse's smile, or,

Do I show contrition in not having fought back earlier?

No longer did I want to live on borrowed time,

In deep fear of the chronic and the terminal,

The roses beside my bed still lay soft but shriveled—

They were bound to me, as I was to them,

So, I took to watering them, consistently in bountifuls,

Watching as their colour hesitantly returned—

A blush, a tremor of red against the deep gray,

Its stem just bending, not broken, refusing to wilt away.

And something in me mirrored that stem,

I imagined myself stringing festive lights once again,

Not on Christmas trees, but,

Across the days that once seemed damned,

Parallels that played on in the relativity of my time—

As it passed by, both in swift strides and a snail's pace,

Like a flame that'd burn the brightest briefly,

But remain witness to eulogies written,

And the steady mounting of urns- a flame, a pyre,

Of my salvation.

Christmas came in whispers now—

Not carols, but the sounds of silence I'd survived,

Not bells, but the thrum of a heart,

That beat back at Death's hypnotic lullaby,

Not gifts wrapped in glitter,

But the sheer gift of taking breath,

Not joy unblemished, but joy that bleeds,

That singes in the wake of pain—

A pain endured by hopes of nostalgia and memories,

Pushing me, toward one more dawn.

And if this is to be my last December,

Then let it not be a disheartening mourn,

Rather, let it be a record of every scar,

That mapped my journey through the dark,

Let it be known I faced the blight—

Not with festivity, but fight,

Not with laughter, but sight,

Sight of what's ahead, why I must survive,

Flickering, failing, but never fading.

For this body is my battlefield, my temple,

Battered, blistered, cancer-scarred,

Yet holy, for it housed a spirit,

Equipped with an indomitable will,

A conscience that ardently refused to depart,

That refused to succumb to the most sinister of maladies—

A sickness, armed and in its selfishness,

Always ready to kill.

Thus, no hymn was sung, yet the rose dared to rise—

Akin to a quiet carol unsung,

Beneath December's melancholic skies.

About the Author

Subbaiah Nuchimanyanda Muthanna, a 22-year-old student at School of Law, CHRIST (Deemed to be University), Bangalore, is a poet, writer and passionate advocate for both the environment and his homeland- Kodag. Having spent his childhood in Kodag and Mysore as well as his formative teenage years in Chennai, Subbaiah's worldview is richly layered with cultural textures and diverse experiences, all of which find their way into his writing.

Born to Nuchimanyanda Giridhargopal Muthanna and Dr. Sujatha Muthanna, Subbaiah is a young man of many talents. Being a singer and dynamic stage performer, he is a key member of his college band *Ek Bun Samosa*, blending music and poetry to evoke emotion and provoke thought. An avid gamer with a love for eSports, especially Valorant, he also has a penchant to explore the deep waters of philosophy.

Beyond poetry, Subbaiah has been active in various arenas—from Moot court competitions and Space settlement design challenges to singing contests and Model United Nations conferences. He remains deeply committed to environmental advocacy, especially in voicing concerns about the ecological fragility of Kodag.

Subbaiah's love for poetry began early, but it is in spoken-word poetry that he truly comes alive. He revels in the rhythm of language, the play of accents, the magic of pauses and the quirkiness of human speech that lends drama to verse. Influenced by poetic giants like Walt Whitman,

Samuel Taylor Coleridge and Sylvia Plath, his work dances between light and shadow, whimsy and grief—reflected in this debut collection of 22 poems, *From Reverie To Requiem*.

This is just the beginning.

For collaborations, conversations, or simply to share a thought, you can reach him at: subbupoet@gmail.com